THESEUS AND THE MINOTAUR

by Scott R. Welvaert

Consultant:
Dr. Laurel Bowman
Department of Greek and Roman Studies
University of Victoria
Victoria, British Columbia

Capstone
press

Mankato, Minnesota

Capstone Press
151 Good Counsel Drive, P.O. Box 669, Mankato, Minnesota 56002
www.capstonepress.com

Library of Congress Cataloging-in-Publication Data
Welvaert, Scott R.
   Theseus and the Minotaur / Scott Welvaert; consultant, Laurel Bowman.
   p. cm.—(World mythology)
   Includes bibliographical references and index.
   ISBN 0-7368-2663-7 (hardcover)
   1. Theseus (Greek mythology)—Juvenile literature. 2. Minotaur (Greek mythology)—
Juvenile literature. [1. Theseus (Greek mythology) 2. Minotaur (Greek mythology)
3. Mythology, Greek.] I. Title. II. Series: World mythology (Mankato, Minn.)
BL820.T5W45 2004
398.2′0938′02—dc22   2003027205

Editorial Credits
Blake A. Hoena, editor; Juliette Peters, series designer; Patrick Dentinger, book designer
   and illustrator; Alta Schaffer and Wanda Winch, photo researchers; Eric Kudalis,
   product planning editor

Photo Credits
Corel, cover (background), 1, 6
Art Resource, NY, 16; Erich Lessing, 10, 18; Réunion des Musées Nationaux, 4
Corbis/Alinari Archives, 8; Araldo de Luca, cover (statue)
Orbital Sciences Corporation, 20
SuperStock, 12; Cummer Museum of Art & Gardens, 14

1 2 3 4 5 6 09 08 07 06 05 04

TABLE OF CONTENTS

Theseus and the Minotaur by Antoine-Louis Barye shows the Greek hero Theseus fighting the Minotaur.

THESEUS AND THE MINOTAUR

Ancient Greeks and Romans told many stories. One popular story was about the Minotaur (MIH-nuh-tor) and a hero named Theseus (THEE-see-uhss).

The Minotaur was a monster. It had the head of a bull and the body of a man. The Minotaur lived in a maze on the island of Crete. The Minotaur ate anyone who entered the maze.

Theseus was from the Greek city of Athens. As a young man, Theseus made the area around Athens safe for travelers. He killed people such as Cercyon (SER-see-on). Cercyon was very strong and challenged people to wrestle him. He beat and killed the people he fought. Theseus was a skilled wrestler and very quick. He fought and killed Cercyon.

Theseus heard about the Minotaur and the people it had eaten. Theseus then knew he had to go on a quest. He had to travel to Crete and kill the Minotaur.

GREEK *and* ROMAN *Mythical Figures*

Greek Name: **AEGEUS**
Roman Name: **AEGEUS**
King of Athens and possibly
Theseus' father

Greek Name: **AETHRA**
Roman Name: **AETHRA**
Theseus' mother

Greek Name: **ARIADNE**
Roman Name: **ARIADNE**
King Minos' daughter who helps
Theseus escape from the labyrinth

Greek Name: **DAEDALUS**
Roman Name: **DAEDALUS**
Builder of the labyrinth

Greek Name: **MINOS**
Roman Name: **MINOS**
King of Crete

Greek Name: **PASIPHAE**
Roman Name: **PASIPHAE**
King Minos' wife and mother of
the Minotaur

Greek Name: **POSEIDON**
Roman Name: **NEPTUNE**
God of the sea and possibly
Theseus' father

Greek Name: **ZEUS**
Roman Name: **JUPITER**
Ruler of the gods

ABOUT MYTHS

The stories told by ancient Greeks and Romans are called myths. Myths are filled with monsters. Some monsters, such as the Minotaur, had human and animal parts. Other monsters had parts from different animals. A griffon (GRIF-uhn) had the head and wings of an eagle and the body of a lion.

Ancient storytellers may have gotten ideas for monsters from things people saw. Long ago, not everyone knew that people rode horses. To some people, a person riding a horse may have looked like a half-human, half-horse monster. This monster was called a centaur (SEN-tor). A centaur had the upper body of a human and the lower body of a horse.

Archaeologists have found many items from ancient Greek and Roman times. Some artifacts show people jumping over bulls. Historians believe priests held rituals where people jumped over bulls. The priests wore bull masks. The idea for the Minotaur may have come from these priests.

In this ancient Roman sculpture, King Minos makes an offering at one of Poseidon's temples.

POSEIDON'S BULL

In myths, King Minos (MYE-nuhss) ruled Crete. This island lies south of Greece in the Mediterranean Sea. People did not think Minos was a good king. He had many enemies.

Minos prayed to the sea god Poseidon (poh-SYE-don) for a large bull. A gift from Poseidon would show Minos' enemies that the sea god supported him. Then Minos' enemies would be afraid to attack him. In return for the gift, Minos said he would sacrifice the bull to honor Poseidon.

Poseidon answered Minos' prayer. He sent the king a large white bull. But King Minos thought the bull was too beautiful to kill. Minos broke his promise. He sacrificed a different bull to Poseidon.

Minos' actions angered Poseidon, and the sea god punished the king. He made Minos' wife, Pasiphae (pa-SIH-fay), fall in love with the white bull.

Giulio Romano painted *Pasiphae and Daedalus*. This painting shows Daedalus helping Pasiphae into the wooden cow he built.

THE MINOTAUR

Pasiphae loved Poseidon's white bull very much. She asked the inventor Daedalus (DEH-duh-luhss) to make her a hollow wooden cow. Pasiphae placed the fake cow in the field where the bull grazed. Then she hid inside the cow. In this way, she could be near the bull.

Pasiphae and the bull had a child. Their child had the head of a bull and the body of a man. It was called the Minotaur.

King Minos hated the Minotaur. He wanted to lock up the monster. He asked Daedalus to build a cage for the Minotaur.

Daedalus built a huge maze. This cage was called the labyrinth (LA-buh-rinth). It had many twists and turns. Only Daedalus knew the way out of the maze. Once the labyrinth was built, Minos put the Minotaur into the maze.

In this etching, seven women are being led to the Minotaur's labyrinth. The women are part of the tribute Athens paid to Crete.

KING MINOS ATTACKS ATHENS

One of King Minos' sons was killed while in the city of Athens. King Minos was angry about his son's death. He went to war with Athens.

The people of Athens fought hard. Minos could not capture the city. So the king prayed to Zeus, the ruler of the gods, for help.

Zeus caused a great hunger and sickness to spread across Athens. Minos attacked the city while its people were weak and sick. He easily took over Athens.

After the war ended, Minos said that he would free Athens under one condition. The people of Athens had to pay Crete a tribute. Every few years, they had to send seven young men and seven young women to Crete. These men and women would be put into the labyrinth. The Minotaur would eat them.

In *Theseus Discovering His Father's Sword* by Reynaud Levieux,
Theseus uncovers the sword and sandals Aegeus hid for him.

THESEUS

King Aegeus (ih-JEE-uhss) ruled Athens. While visiting the town of Troezen, he fell in love with Aethra (IH-thruh). Poseidon also loved Aethra.

Aethra had a son, Theseus. Some myths say Aegeus is Theseus' father. Other myths say that his father is Poseidon.

Before leaving Troezen, Aegeus hid a pair of sandals and a sword under a heavy stone. He told Aethra that Theseus must try to lift the stone when he grew up. If Theseus could, then he should go to Athens and become king.

As a young man, Theseus easily lifted the stone. He took the sword and sandals and traveled to Athens.

When Theseus arrived in Athens, Aegeus did not recognize him. The king was going to have Theseus killed. But then Aegeus saw Theseus' sword. Aegeus knew it was the sword he left under the stone. He knew Theseus was his son.

Theseus and the Minotaur by Master of the Campana Cassone shows scenes from Theseus' adventures. On the left, Theseus (in armor) meets Ariadne. On the right, he battles the Minotaur in the maze.

THESEUS GOES TO CRETE

Theseus heard about the tribute Athens paid to Crete. He did not like it that young people from Athens were killed by the Minotaur. Theseus joined the third group of men and women sent to Crete. Once there, he hoped to kill the Minotaur.

When they arrived in Crete, the young men and women from Athens were put in a cage. King Minos' daughter Ariadne (ah-ree-AD-nee) saw Theseus among them. She fell in love with him. Ariadne wanted to help Theseus.

Ariadne went to Daedalus for help. Daedalus gave her a spool of thread. He told Ariadne how the thread could be used to escape the labyrinth.

Ariadne then made a deal with Theseus. She said she would help him. But in return, Theseus had to take her away from Crete and marry her. Theseus agreed. Ariadne gave Theseus the thread, so he could escape the labyrinth. She also gave him a sword to kill the Minotaur.

This ancient Greek vase shows Theseus killing the Minotaur. Greeks decorated everyday items, such as vases, cups, and bowls, with scenes from myths.

THESEUS KILLS THE MINOTAUR

Guards led Theseus and the other young men and women into the labyrinth. Theseus tied the end of the thread to the labyrinth's entrance. He traveled through many dark hallways and around many corners. As he walked, he unraveled the thread.

Theseus found the Minotaur in the deepest, darkest part of the labyrinth. The area was covered with bones from the people the monster had killed. There, Theseus fought and killed the Minotaur.

Afterward, Theseus led the men and women out of the labyrinth. He simply followed the thread back to the entrance. He was the first person to find his way out of the maze.

Then Theseus and the men and women from Athens sailed home. The people of Athens never had to pay another tribute to Crete.

Ariadne went with Theseus. But Theseus did not want to marry her. He visited the island of Naxos and left Ariadne there.

Minotaur rockets are used to launch satellites into space.

Today, many things are named after people and creatures from myths. The ship Theseus sailed to Crete had black sails. For the trip back to Athens, Aegeus told Theseus to use white sails if he had killed the Minotaur. But the gods made Theseus forget to change the sails because he did not keep his promise to marry Ariadne. When Aegeus saw the ship returning with black sails, he thought Theseus had been killed by the Minotaur. Out of sadness, the king jumped into the sea and died. The sea he died in was named the Aegean Sea.

The Orbital Sciences Corporation builds large rockets called Minotaurs. Minotaur rockets have been used to launch satellites into space.

People no longer believe that Greek and Roman myths are true. Still, people enjoy them. Myths are exciting stories about heroes and monsters, such as Theseus and the Minotaur.

Adriatic Sea

•Rome

ITALY

N
W • E
S

•Troy

GREECE

Aegean Sea

Ionian Sea

Athens•

Troezen•

Sparta•

—NAXOS

SICILY

LEGEND

• City

Mount Olympus

CRETE

SCALE

Miles

0   100   200

0   100   200

Kilometers

Mediterranean Sea

GLOSSARY

ancient (AYN-shunt)—having lived a long time ago, or very old

archaeologist (ar-kee-AW-luh-jist)—a scientist who digs up and studies items used by people who lived a long time ago

artifact (ART-tuh-fakt)—an item used by people who lived a long time ago

centaur (SEN-tor)—a monster with the upper body of a human and the lower body of a horse

griffon (GRIF-uhn)—a monster with the head, front legs, and wings of an eagle and the body, back legs, and tail of a lion

quest (KWEST)—a journey taken by a hero to perform a task

ritual (RIH-chuh-wuhl)—a set of actions performed as part of a religious ceremony or social custom

sacrifice (SAK-ruh-fisse)—to kill an animal in order to honor a god

satellite (SAT-uh-lite)—a spacecraft that orbits earth

tribute (TRIB-yoot)—a payment

READ MORE

Fanelli, Sara. *Mythological Monsters of Ancient Greece.* Cambridge, Mass.: Candlewick Press, 2002.

Spinner, Stephanie. *Monster in the Maze: The Story of the Minotaur.* All Aboard Reading. New York: Grosset & Dunlap, 2000.

USEFUL ADDRESSES

National Junior Classical League
422 Wells Mill Drive
Miami University
Oxford, OH 45056

Ontario Classical Association
PO Box 19505
55 Bloor Street West
Toronto, ON M4W 3T9
Canada

INTERNET SITES

FactHound offers a safe, fun way to find Internet sites related to this book. All of the sites on FactHound have been researched by our staff.

Here's how:
1. Visit *www.facthound.com*
2. Type in this special code **0736826637** for age-appropriate sites. Or enter a search word related to this book for a more general search.
3. Click on the **Fetch It** button.

FactHound will fetch the best sites for you!

INDEX